NEOSOUL**JAZZ** **GUITAR**SOLOING

Learn to Combine The Language of Bebop and Neosoul in Modern Fusion Guitar Solos

MARK**WHITFIELD**

FUNDAMENTAL**CHANGES**

NeoSoul Jazz Guitar Soloing

Learn to Combine The Language of Bebop and NeoSoul in Modern Fusion Guitar Solos

ISBN: 978-1-78933-251-3

Published by **www.fundamental-changes.com**

www.fundamental-changes.com

Over 12,000 fans on Facebook: **FundamentalChangesInGuitar**

Instagram: **FundamentalChanges**

For over 350 Free Guitar Lessons with Videos Check Out

www.fundamental-changes.com

Cover Image Copyright: Author photo by Deneka Peniston, used with permission

Track credits:

Chapter One: Cali, ItsWatR

Chapter Two: Pixabay audio

Chapter Three: Mirage, tobylane

Chapter Four: Pixabay audio

Chapter Five: Essence, tobylane

Chapter Six: Organic Lo Fi, Coma-Media

Contents

About the Author

Mark Whitfield graduated from Boston's prestigious Berklee College of Music, the world's foremost institution for the study of Jazz and modern American music, in the spring of 1987. Shortly thereafter, he returned to his to his native New York to embark on a career as a jazz guitarist that has afforded him the opportunity to collaborate with such legendary artists as Dizzy Gillespie, Art Blakey, Quincy Jones, Ray Charles, Herbie Hancock, Carmen McRae, Gladys Knight, Burt Bacharach, Jimmy Smith, Clark Terry, Shirley Horn, Wynton Marsalis, Branford Marsalis, Joe Williams, Stanley Turrentine, and his mentor, the great George Benson.

In 1990 the New York Times dubbed Whitfield "The Best Young Guitarist in the Business". Later that year, Warner Bros. released his debut album, *The Marksman*. The success of his debut release led to a recording career that has produced a total of 16 solo recordings and myriad collaborative efforts with some of the most important artists in recent years including Sting, Steven Tyler, D'Angelo, Mary J. Blige, John Mayer, Chaka Khan, Jill Scott, Diana Krall, Christian McBride, Chris Botti, Roy Hargrove, Nicholas Payton and Robert Glasper.

Mark remains extremely active as a performer, recording artist and sideman, and is a highly sought-after instructor and master clinician. 2022 will see the release of his newest recording, *GBD*, which features fellow jazz legends bassist Robert Hurst and drummer Jeff "Tain" Watts.

Introduction: What is Neo-Soul Guitar?

It can be a little hard to describe Neo-Soul as a genre of music, since it's really a melting pot of a number of diverse musical forms. It emerged as a mixture of Soul and contemporary RnB, but soon became infused with influences from Jazz, Funk, Fusion, Hip-Hop, African music, and Electronic music.

The term was first coined by American producer Kedar Massenburg (president of Motown Records from 1997-2004), who wanted a phrase to describe a genre that acknowledged the influence of Hip-Hop and other electronic musical styles but, at the same time, was a return to earlier forms of Soul music.

At the time, Massenburg had signed breakthrough artist Erykah Badu who somewhat defied categorization. Along with other critical artists of the early 90s, such as D'Angelo (who I had the pleasure of recording with), Lauren Hill and Maxwell, the foundations of Neo-Soul were laid. In particular, the success of D'Angelo's 1995 album *Brown Sugar* was pivotal in bringing the sound of Neo-Soul to the masses.

Neo-Soul suffered a decline in the mid-to-late 2000s, but since 2010 onwards has enjoyed a massive resurgence through artists such as Jill Scott, John Legend, Amy Winehouse, Leela James, Raheem DeVaughn and Mayer Hawthorne, to name just a few.

One of the most interesting things to me about the Neo-Soul revival is how the guitar has played an increasingly important role in the music, and how social media platforms such as Instagram have spawned many great players who are passionate about this music. Check out the playing of Todd Pritchard, Kerry "2Smooth" Marshall, Isaiah Sharkey and Mark Lettieri for examples of players who are pioneering this style today. So many more could be mentioned!

My background is in jazz guitar, but I've always had an association with Neo-Soul and a love for this style of music. Jazz blends easily with Neo-Soul and, with this in mind, I wanted to put together a resource for guitarists that teaches the *language* of Neo-Soul jazz guitar in an easily accessible manner.

As a guitar style, it is still emerging, and I wanted to push the boundaries a little further in terms of applying jazz techniques to create some exciting lines. I hope the ideas here help you to see the possibilities of this genre of music, and also just help you to become a better musician.

Lots of Neo-Soul music is heavily groove based and often features multiple bars of static chords or short progressions that loop around a main tonal center. It made sense, therefore, to present you with Neo-Soul vocabulary in the form of a collection of licks/phrases that you can play over minor, major and dominant grooves to help you master the language.

The Neo-Soul Jazz Guitarist's Toolkit

Throughout this book, while I will give you a breakdown of every single lick, pointing out any special techniques and specific points of interest, I also want to point you toward the stylistic traits that *sum up* the sound of Neo-Soul guitar. Throughout the text, I'll refer to these musical choices that I call the Neo-Soul guitarist's "toolkit" and you'll learn how to apply them.

As well as the audio to every example, full-length backing tracks accompany this book, so you can practice and develop these techniques for yourself.

If we breakdown the techniques commonly used in Neo-Soul guitar, the following ideas feature most often:

Blues licks

With its RnB/Soul roots, the blues is never far from Neo-Soul, but here it is applied in a cool, laidback manner. This might include lazy, behind-the-beat phrases, call and response phrases, and vocal-like articulation. A defining feature of the blues is the blurring of the minor/major tonality, often expressed by playing both minor and major pentatonic ideas over a minor blues and vice versa. This idea can also be used in Neo-Soul as you'll discover in Chapter One.

Double-Stops

The use of double-stops is an idea that crops up in all kinds of guitar music from Rock to Country to Blues and is a technique that really works well in Neo-Soul over its spacious grooves. Funky double-stops with a strong rhythm are often effective in this style of playing.

Motifs

The idea of developing motifs occurs in many musical genres but is a key skill in jazz soloing. A motif is a simple musical phrase that is stated, then repeated and developed. It's similar to the idea of the "call and response" in Blues but finds more freedom of expression in Jazz. Playing a motif, then building on the initial idea and developing it, gives your improvisations a sense of purpose and direction. It's a tried and tested technique every great player has used to add the vital element of storytelling to a solo.

Rhythmic phrasing

The groove-based nature of Neo-Soul calls out for strong rhythmic phrasing from the guitar player. This can range from applying syncopated rhythms to simple phrases to make them pop out, to creating polyrhythmic riffs, such as playing groups of triplets over a 4/4 groove to create a three-over-four feel.

Long lines

One great idea that is Charlie Parker's legacy to the jazz community is allowing melodic lines to flow over the music, crossing the bar lines. Parker would often play lines that began mid-bar and ended in the middle of the bar a few measures later. It made his lines more musical and less predictable. Since a lot of Neo-Soul is based around looping progressions and tonal centers, this idea can work really well, so at times you'll hear me play lines that are complete phrases in themselves but start/end partway through a bar and flow across the bar lines.

Chromatic passing notes

Finally, another idea borrowed from Jazz is the use of extended or chromatic passing notes. In laying the foundations of bebop, Charlie Parker pioneered the idea of targeting chord tones with approach notes from above or below.

Sometimes these notes would be extensions of the chord he was playing over – e.g. over a G7 chord he might highlight the 9th, 11th or 13th extended tones – and sometimes they would be chromatic passing notes i.e. notes not belonging to the parent key. Over a G7 chord, chromatic passing notes could imply altered tones such as the b5, #5, b9 and #9.

You can take a lot of liberties with this idea as long as you keep the "home" tonality of the tune in mind. Playing longer chromatic lines is a great way to create an "outside-inside" sound, as long as you resolve your idea to a strong chord tone that allows the listener to keep connected to the harmony.

Look out for all of these techniques as we progress through the book.

Lastly, a word on learning. Whenever you hear a lick you really like, practice it until you've committed it to memory. Once you have the sound and shape of it down, play it in different octaves then transpose it to other keys. Working with an idea like this is a proven way to absorb it into your musical vocabulary. Also feel free to adapt and change up these ideas. By all means take the seed of an idea and alter it so that it sounds more like you.

Above all, enjoy your playing because that's what music is all about. Now it's time to learn some licks. Have fun!

Mark Whitfield

New York City

Get the Audio

The audio files for this book are available to download for free from **www.fundamental-changes.com.** The link is in the top right-hand corner. Click on the "Guitar" link then simply select this book title from the drop-down menu and follow the instructions to get the audio.

We recommend that you download the files directly to your computer, not to your tablet, and extract them there before adding them to your media library. You can then put them onto your tablet, iPod or burn them to CD. On the download page there are instructions and we also provide technical support via the contact form.

For over 350 free guitar lessons with videos check out:

www.fundamental-changes.com

Over 12,000 fans on Facebook: **FundamentalChangesInGuitar**

Tag us for a share on Instagram: **FundamentalChanges**

Chapter One – C Minor Groove

In this chapter we're going to work with a groove that has a tonal center of C Minor. Most of this tune is a straight vamp that loops around, with a slight variation that acts as a short bridge later on. As we progress, I'll explain the approach I used to conceive each lick and point out relevant scale or note choices.

The first four examples all use the idea of developing a motif. Motifs typically start quite simple and can consist of just a few notes. As they develop, they can become more complex, but the listener should still be able to identify the seed of the idea that began the improvisation. The restatement of the original melodic idea is what gives the music continuity. It helps you tell a story with your music, rather than playing unconnected musical ideas.

Here's a simple idea to get us started. It has an element of the "question and answer" phrasing of the Blues to it.

Example 1a

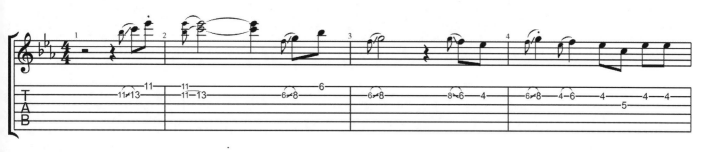

This line creates a motif around the Eb note on the third string, 8th fret. It's the b3 of the underlying Cm7 chord, so is a very strong note, rooted in the harmony. By bar four, the motif has developed into a melody.

Example 1b

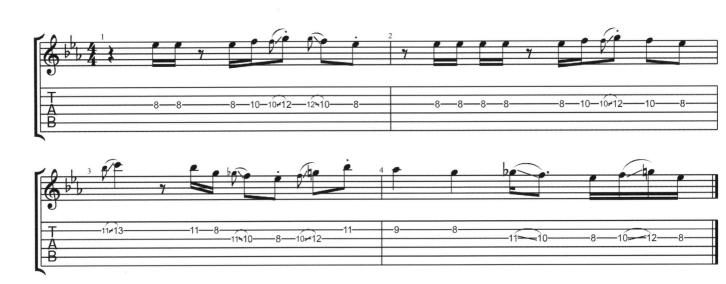

Example 1c is built around the same motif, but then takes it in a different direction, turning it into a bluesy phrase. I used the C Blues scale in bar three (C, Eb, F, Gb, G, Bb). The Gb note used throughout creates the classic bluesy b5 sound.

Example 1c

The final motif lick combines several ideas from the Neo-Soul toolkit.

First, the motif is a little more complex than the previous ideas and begins partway through a bar.

Second, I added the idea of *rhythmic displacement* i.e. playing the same (or a similar) idea beginning on a different beat of the bar. In bar two the motif is stated after a 1/16th note rest. In bar three it begins right on beat 1.

Third, in bar four, I broke up the rhythm of the line by mixing up 1/8th note triplets with straight 1/8th notes and 1/16th note triplets. This idea gives the line a rhythmic surprise and stops it from sounding too predictable.

Example 1d

For the next few examples we're going to dig further into the Blues area of our toolbox. One of the defining characteristics of the Blues is how soloists move between major and minor sounds over the same progression. It's very common to play both major and minor pentatonic licks, for example, whether playing over a major- or minor-key blues.

In bar three of Example 1e, the C Blues scale is implied, but I also highlight the major 3rd (E) to blur the boundaries between minor and major and create a more interesting sound.

Example 1e

This line opens simply by stating the root and b3 of Cm7, clearly laying down the tonal center. The next part of the phrase combines an A note borrowed from C Major Pentatonic with a chromatic run down to the 5th of Cm7.

On beat 3 of bar two, a slide from 1st to 2nd fret on the fourth string highlights the minor to major 3rd sound again. The same idea happens in bar three, which uses notes from the C Natural Minor scale (C, D, Eb, F, G, Ab, Bb) with the addition of the major 3rd (E).

Example 1f

Here's one more example of this idea developed into a more complex line. Throughout, a passing E note is used to emphasize the major 3rd sound. Look out for the change in rhythmic phrasing in bar three, where straight 1/16th notes transition into 1/16th note sextuplets, then back to straight 1/16th notes. Slow this line down and work out your fingering and picking patterns before bringing it up to tempo.

Example 1g

The next lick is based around the C Natural Minor scale (C, D, Eb, F, G, Ab, Bb) and includes some bluesy double-stop ideas that are common Neo-Soul vocabulary. That's the thing about Neo-Soul – it's soulful and bluesy, but it's not pure, traditional blues – it has a richer harmonic palette.

Example 1h

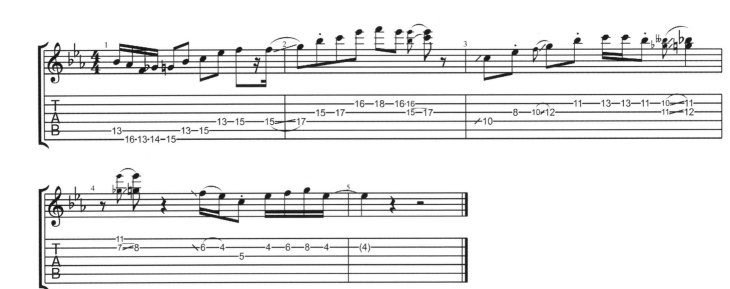

This line uses a Gb to G movement several times. I think of the Gb as a chromatic approach note, but it could also be seen as coming from the C Blues scale. In this example I briefly use my trademark fast alternate picking to create surprise and interest in bar one, and there are several more of the double-stop phrases that work so well in this genre of music.

Example 1i

14

Implied harmony

If I find myself soloing over a static tonal center for an extended period, I'll imagine a progression happening that I can imply with my melodic lines. When playing over a C minor vamp I might, for example, view that chord as though it's part of a progression, even though the other chords are not written on the lead sheet.

For instance, I might visualize Cm7 in the context of a minor ii V i (Dm7b5 – G7alt – Cm7). With those additional chords in mind, I'll create a harmonic palette from which I can draw my melodic lines. Visualizing this enhanced harmony gives me alternative note choices and colors to use.

In this next example, I imagined that the progression was a G7alt chord resolving to Cm7. To play over an altered dominant chord, jazz musicians will often superimpose a minor scale a half step above its root note.

Playing Ab Melodic Minor over G7alt is a common choice, the effect of which is to create the G Altered scale (G, Ab, Bb, B, Db, Eb, F) and highlight all the altered dominant tension notes (b5, #5, b9, #9).

However, you can use other Ab minor sounds as well, for a similar result.

This is the thought process that led me to play notes from Ab Melodic Minor, and also Ab Natural Minor and Ab Blues scales over a Cm7 chord! The result is an outside sound that will eventually resolve to the "home" sound of C minor.

In bar four I move away from the scale superimposition idea, but I'm still thinking of the implied harmony of a G7 chord. The first four notes are the end of my Ab Melodic Minor phrase, but the rest of the notes are all G Mixolydian. The line resolves on the very last note of the phrase – a D, implying a Cm9 sound.

Example 1j

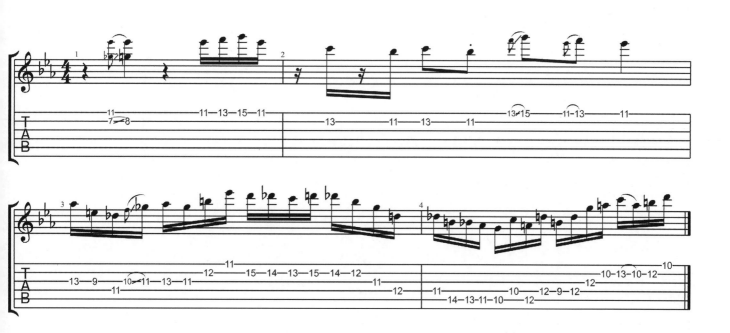

When I play a line, I'll always have a starting point and end target in mind. The beginning point could come from the underlying Cm7 or an implied chord, but the target will usually be a strong chord tone from the parent key. In between the start and the target, I'll have in mind a clear way of reaching my destination. It could be a motif that moves and repeats, or simply some chromatic notes that move outside the harmony before resolving.

Keep in mind that your lines should have a clear beginning, middle and end, and you'll just play better lines! Jazz is all about the phrasing, and we want to avoid playing lines that start well then fade, or don't have any strong direction.

The next line begins with harmonic targeting, with chromatic notes targeting Cm7 chord tones, then it develops into a melodic motif.

Example 1k

In the next example, I'm thinking "minor ii V i (Dm7b5 – G7alt – Cm7) and the shape of the line reflects this. Play those chords along with the lick and you'll get the idea. Throughout the line I've used occasional chromatic notes to join the dots and keep the line flowing, but essentially bar one is D Locrian (Dm7b5), bar two is G Altered (G7alt) and the line resolves to an F note in bar three (the 11th of C minor to create a cool Cm11 sound).

Example 1l

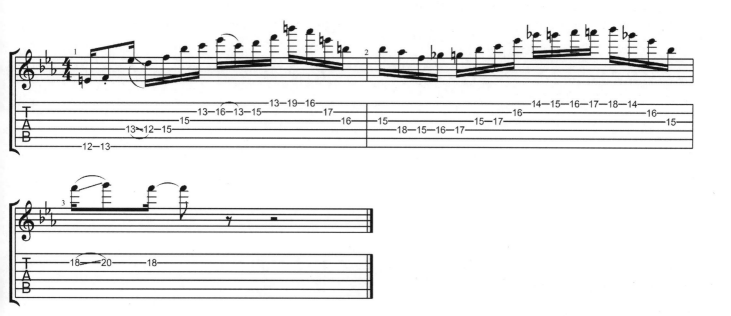

Bar one of the next lick shows an example of harmonic targeting. The line has a clear starting point (the G chord tone on the first string 15th fret, which is the 5th of Cm7), an idea for the middle that will move us toward the destination (a short motif followed by a descending line), and an end target (to hit the G chord tone again on beat 1 of bar two). Notice that the destination becomes the launch pad for the next melodic idea in bar two.

Example 1m

At the beginning of the next line, I'm thinking of the C Natural Minor scale with added chromatic passing notes. The opening ten-note phrase begins with the b7 of Cm7 but ends with an extended chord tone (b13) for a more unpredictable sound.

In bar two, I'm now thinking C Melodic Minor and adding some passing notes to target a strong G chord tone exactly on beat 4.

Example 1n

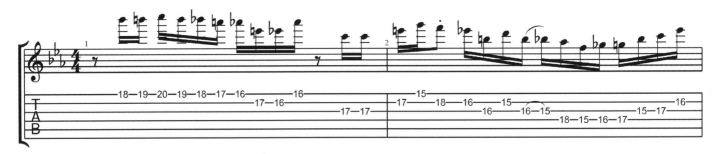

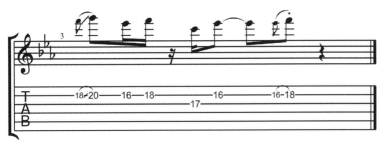

In the next couple of examples, I want to demonstrate how you can "stretch" the idea of achieving good phrasing for your melodic ideas over several bars. The principle remains the same: we need a clear beginning, middle and end, but we have to work a little harder to maintain interest and momentum as we head for the target.

In Example 1o I'm visualizing a different implied harmony. Here, I'm viewing the Cm7 as though it's chord ii in a ii V I in Bb Major. In this context, most of the note choices will come from the C Dorian scale (C, D, Eb, F, G, A, Bb).

In bar one, I'm using the notes of this scale to form a short motif. As the motif repeats, you can hear that each statement sounds like an arpeggio. From bar one to beat 3 of bar two, they spell out G minor, Cm9 (without a root), Fsus and F6(add11). Each of these chords belong to the implied parent key of Bb Major.

During bars 3-4 my focus was using C Dorian to target some strong Cm7 chord tones, using the occasional passing note.

In bar five, to change things up, I switch to C Melodic Minor (C, D, Eb, F, G, A, B) briefly before moving into the C Blues scale to begin to close out the lick. The line ends with a double-stop.

Example 1o

The next line is a variation on the previous idea. For most of this lick I was thinking in terms of C Dorian with the addition of some passing notes, apart from in bar three which uses the G Altered scale with an added C passing note.

Example 1p

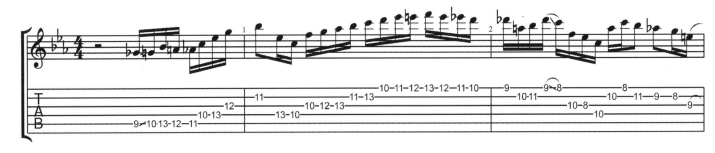

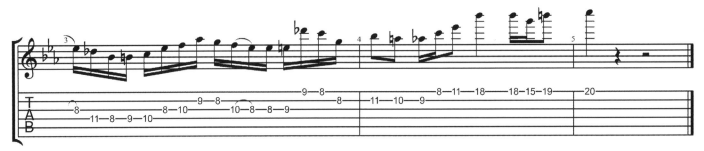

To end this chapter, here are a couple of rhythmic ideas. I often get asked about my fast picking technique, so here are two examples that use it.

The secret here is just fast alternate down-up picking, but to get it fast you must first practice it slow! In order to play fast, it's really about locking good picking motion into muscle memory. Play slowly at first and make sure that your picking action is both *economical* (don't move the pick more than you need to) and *consistent* (aim to strike the string with the same amount of force with every stroke and with good timing).

Check it out!

Example 1q

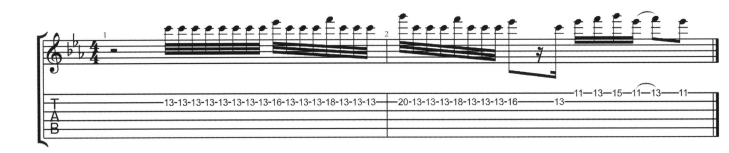

Here's a slightly different take. Don't speed it up until you can play the phrase very cleanly at a slower tempo. In order to develop this technique during practice times, use a metronome and increase the tempo in small increments until you're pushing yourself to the edge of your ability. If you persist with this, the speed will come.

Example 1r

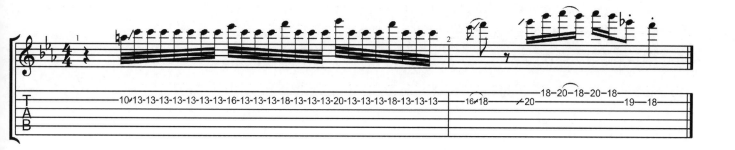

Chapter Two – A Minor Groove

We continue our exploration of Neo-Soul vocabulary with a tune in the key of A Minor. Here, the core progression cycles around these changes:

| F G | Am7 | F G | Dm7 |

For this tune, my melodic thinking is based primarily around diatonic scales, mainly A Aeolian (A B C D E F G i.e. a C Major scale starting and ending on A), but I also use the A Blues and A Minor Pentatonic scales for variety. To spice up the lines, I will also typically add in diatonic passing notes (to extend the harmony) and chromatic passing notes in jazz-style enclosures.

For a more "outside" sound, I'll occasionally use *side-stepping*. This technique involves playing a melodic phrase that begins a half step above or below an A Minor scale position but resolves to the home key.

Now let's get into the licks.

A key technique in Neo-Soul is the use of double-stops to create musical phrases that fill out the sound, which works well over the sometimes sparse backing. I think of this technique as a nod to the Soul roots of the music and several of the examples that follow will use this idea.

In Example 2a, the idea is to play sliding double-stops that transition into a hammer-on. The notes are drawn from the A Minor Pentatonic scale (A C D E G). In bar three, I change up the double-stop approach slightly in the higher register and alternate the direction of the slides to create some melodic variety in the phrase.

Double-stop phrases are a great "way in" to a solo and are often an effective way to begin. Note the combination of 1/8th and 1/16th note rhythms in bar three, which really help the phrase to "sing". They should be played in a laid-back, "lazy" manner.

Example 2a

Next, here is a predominantly single note line. I often like to use a combination of bluesy phrasing and rapid-fire picking like this. Avoiding playing on the first beat of each bar adds a more vocal quality to the phrasing of the line. Also note the triplet-based rhythms in each bar that help the line to swing.

Rhythmic punctuation is important in crafting soulful ideas and the double-stop in bar two is a great example of how this can be applied in Neo-Soul. In bar three, I'm playing the major third to deliberately blur the minor/major tonality, just like a blues player would.

Example 2b

Example 2c has a strong swing feel to the rhythm and is a great example of the "call and response" approach to phrasing used by many Neo-Soul players. The first phrase (call) is punctuated by a double-stop in bar two. To give the response a more vocal-like articulation in bar three, the phrasing has some subtle finger slides. This is also an example of allowing phrases to flow across the bar lines, and leaving space, which adds to the vocal quality.

Example 2c

Here is another double-stop call and response idea. This time using the A Aeolian scale, the line begins with a series of double-stops in diatonic 3rds. To break up this idea, I play a single note phrase in bar two before returning to double-stops in bar three.

As with the previous example, pay particular attention to the small slides being used here. They may seem subtle, but they go a long way to making the phrases sound more musical.

Example 2d also highlights the use of a motif. Compare bars two and four, where an almost note-for-note repeat occurs with slight variations.

Example 2d

Example 2e illustrates just how much melodic variety you can achieve with even the smallest phrase variation. Listen to the audio to grasp the time-feel I'm using here. I deliberately play behind the beat to create a more laid-back feel.

This is a technique used by many jazz players, who will alternate between playing slightly behind and slightly in front of the beat. This *pulling* and *pushing* effect is what makes the music swing.

Time spent soloing against a metronome will pay dividends in your practice sessions to develop this technique. Over time, you'll begin to hear the beat as the "center" of the groove and understand how to place notes fractionally either side of it.

Example 2e

This example emphasizes behind the beat phrasing even more. If you struggle to get this, I suggest deliberately playing lazily over the pulse of the music.

Guitar players often have the tendency to speed up when playing, but record yourself playing "late" and you may be surprised at the results. Phrasing behind the beat always sounds more natural in Neo-Soul and is a very commonplace rhythmic approach in this style of music.

This lick also leaves space between phrases to make them stand out more, and there are some double-stop/ hammer-on combinations for a more fluid sound.

Example 2f

Next, we're going to move on to look at some faster, flowing lines. Some of these ideas are more challenging to play and they lean harder into the bebop side of my playing.

Example 2g uses combinations of 1/16th note triplets and also includes a string skipping idea in bar one. It may take a little practice to nail the exact phrasing I'm using here, but the core idea is to create a fast fluid line that cuts against the groove, so feel free to adapt and make this your own.

The line ascends the fretboard rapidly, then descends by using a melodic figure that uses the same intervals through three full octaves. This approach can create a lot of drama in a line and is a great contrast to the double-stops and more bluesy ideas of earlier examples.

Example 2g

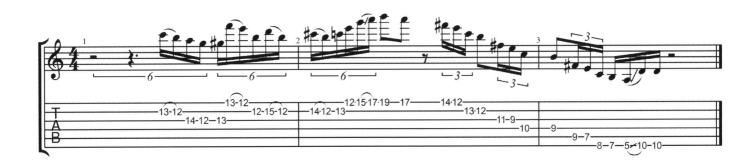

The next lick is all about rhythmic phrasing and includes some "outside" playing towards the end of the line. I'm mostly using 1/16th notes here but notice how they are played across the bar lines in sequential fashion.

In my musical career, I've had the immense privilege of playing with legends such as Dizzy Gillespie and Stanley Turrentine, and this kind of lick is an homage to their influence and their ability to play long legato lines.

Here, diatonic passing notes emphasize specific intervals including the 9th and 11th over the underlying A minor harmony. In the final bar, I break with the diatonic harmony briefly by using a C# triad to create some strong harmonic tension. It's an example of side-stepping – approaching the tonal center from a half step above.

Example 2h

Combining different rhythmic groupings can add a lot of musical color to a solo and in this next example I've used groupings of both six and seven notes over the space of a 1/4 note. The lick begins with a bluesy high register double-stop phrase, which employs a common tone on the first string, fret 17.

In bar two, I begin a long, fast bebop style line which makes use of chromatic passing notes. Practice this slowly and work out an economical fingering that is comfortable for you. You might find it helpful to break down the longest phrase into smaller sections.

Example 2i

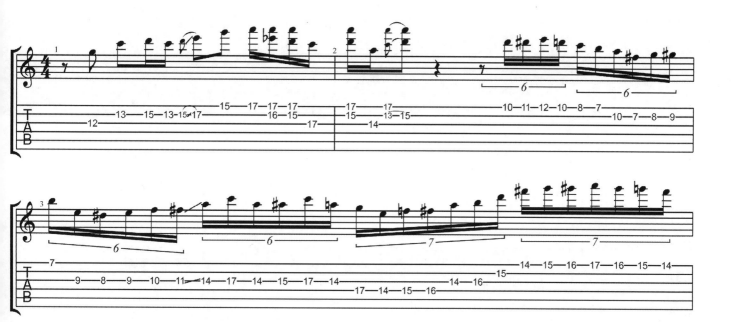

Example 2j launches with a bluesy 1/8th and 1/16th note phrase that ends with the double-stop midway through bar three. From here, I change my melodic thinking from a scalic to an arpeggio-based approach.

When playing over a static chord, jazz musicians will often use other arpeggios diatonic to the parent key for soloing. When the A Natural Minor scale is harmonized (stacked in intervals of a 3rd), it produces the following set of chords:

Am7, Bm7b5, Cmaj7, Dm7, Em7, Fmaj7, G7

Our underlying harmony is A minor, but we can superimpose any other arpeggio from the parent key over that chord. In bar three, for instance, I'm spelling out Fmaj7, Am7 and Cmaj7 arpeggios, concluding the line on the 5th interval of the chord.

Each superimposed arpeggio has a different effect on the underlying Am7 chord.

Am7 has the notes A C E G.

Fmaj7 shares three of those notes and adds an F. Over Am7, the F note implies an Am7b13 sound.

Cmaj7 also shares three notes with Am7 and adds a B. Over Am7, it implies an Am9 sound.

Though I don't use it here, also check out the effect of playing the Bm7b5 arpeggio over Am7. It has the notes B D F A, respectively the 9th, 11th, b13 and root over A minor. It's a cool sound!

Example 2j

The next example begins with a repeated motif using 1/16th note triplets. As in previous examples, I use several finger slides to avoid sounding too staccato and there are also some string skips to navigate.

Example 2k

Here is another fast-picked line for you to dig into. Break it down into smaller sections to learn it. It has a lot of 1/16th note triplet figures and uses chromatic passing notes to retain the long, unbroken line. Prepare for the quick position shift at the end of the line so you can make that final slide up to the 19th fret.

Example 2l

Example 2m begins with a burst of fast picking that transitions into some soulful bluesy high register phrases. Listen to the audio to catch the rhythmic articulation of each phrase and notice especially the space between phrases in bars 2-4. It can be dramatic to play fast, but never be afraid of space. Short rests between phrases make them sound more musical.

Example 2m

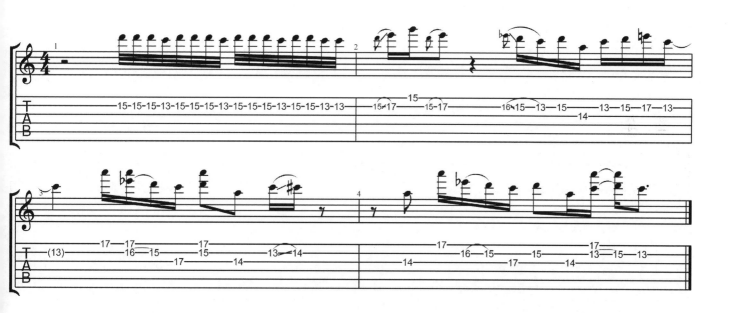

This next line is all about developing a motif over several bars. You'll hear a lot of vocalists and horn players use this approach in Neo-Soul as it's a great way to extend an idea. Note the use of double-stops and hammer-ons to periodically punctuate the phrases in each bar. I'm also playing a little bit more behind the beat here to really make things swing.

Example 2n

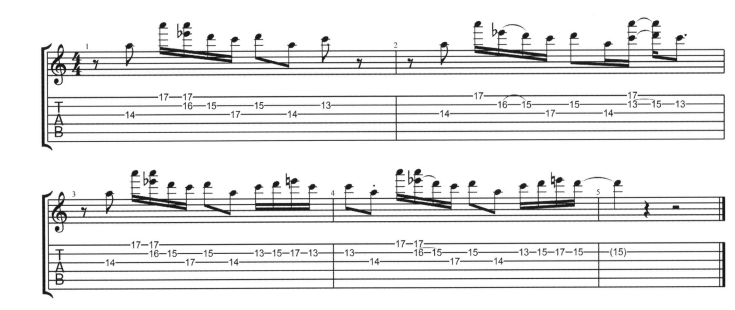

In Example 2o, I begin with a short melodic scale sequence in bar one, adding in a G# chromatic note to resolve to the A tonic note at the beginning of bar two. Using short sequential phrases will add a melodic edge to your soloing and can work effectively in contrast to more bluesy phrases. Many horn players use this idea to achieve a balance in their playing.

Example 2o

Our next line begins in 12th position and quickly moves outside with a Db major triad idea on beat 3. It's another side-step idea, this time approaching the tonal center from a half step below. In bars 2-4 we move into bebop territory with a long line that features lots of passing notes. You can hear just how effectively chromatic jazz lines can work over a static chord in this style of music, especially when played as continuous 1/16th notes.

Example 2p

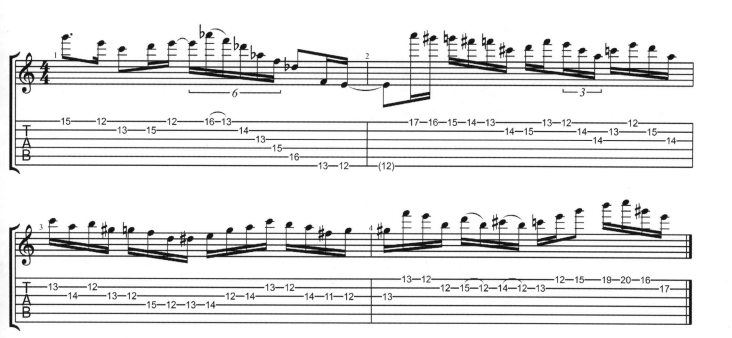

The final example of this chapter is all about rhythmic variety in a line that combines 1/8th notes with straight and triplet 1/16th notes. I begin with a 1/4 note on beat 1 of bar one and gradually increase the rhythmic subdivisions from there. For contrast, the line concludes with a series of sliding double-stops.

Example 2q

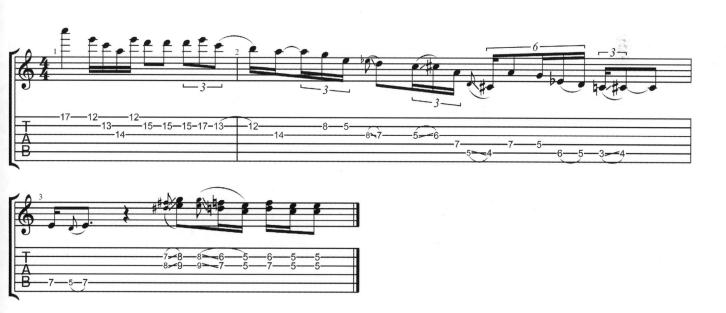

Chapter Three – Ab Major/F Minor Groove

In this chapter we explore some new sonic territory with a groove that cycles between two chords, neither of which are the tonic chord of the key. I chose this track because it exemplifies the approach of Neo-Soul, where sometimes the direction of the harmony is not obvious, and the focus is much more on how the track *feels* than where it's going musically.

The chords flip between Dbmaj7 and the altered dominant chord C7#5. The overall "sound" of the piece suggests that the tonal center is Ab Major/F Minor, though both keys contain a C minor rather than a C dominant 7 chord. However, in Neo-Soul (as in Jazz) it's very common to change the quality of a chord to suit a particular harmonic context, as is the case here.

Because the I chord is never played, this tune has a restless, unresolved feeling to it. This "open" sound led me to use a variety of melodic approaches when constructing my lines. Try these ideas for yourself when jamming over the backing track.

First, we can simply focus on spelling out the chord tones of Dbmaj7 and C7#5.

Second, we can use appropriate scales or modes to outline the harmony.

In the examples that follow, depending on the kind of sound I was aiming for, I used either the straight Db Major scale over the Dbmaj7, treating the chord as a tonal center in its own right, or Db Lydian (Db Eb F G Ab Bb C) to imply the overarching Ab Major tonality.

For the C7#5 chord, I most often turned to the C Altered scale.

C Altered (C Db Eb E Gb Ab Bb) is the seventh mode of Db Melodic Minor and applying it in this context opens up the possibility of moving from Db *major* to *minor* ideas, which is a simple move to make on guitar. That said, over the C7#5 chord you will also hear me use the C Blues scale at times.

We kick off with a simple but effective idea in Example 3a that uses tremolo-picked octaves. Make sure that the second string is effectively muted, then strum down and up rapidly with the picking hand. Check out the audio to hear how it should sound.

The idea here is to ascend gradually to the E octave at the 12th fret, which is the major 3rd of the underlying C7#5 chord. Using a simple device like this is a straightforward but musically satisfying way of indicating the harmony. Playing in octaves, Wes Montgomery-style, also thickens out the guitar part.

Example 3a

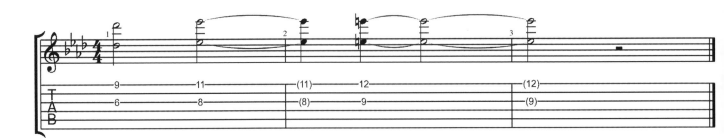

Building on the previous example, here's another octave line played with rhythmic syncopation. Hopefully, you can hear how even very small rhythmic variations can really bring a phrase to life. Notice how I use tied 1/8th notes in bar two, then 1/4 note triplets in bars three and four. Quarter note triplets have the effect of pulling back the time slightly and can be used anywhere you'd like to achieve a more laidback feel.

Like the double-stop examples of the previous chapter, I tend to articulate my octaves with small slides (especially seen in bars 2-4), which adds to the fluid soulful feel.

Example 3b

Before we move on, let's play one more line built from syncopated octaves. This time they are used as part of a call and response phrase. I've also added extra sliding articulation to this line to make the phrasing smoother and more vocal-like.

It's also important to note where I'm *not* playing here. The phrases are given room to breathe, most notably in bars 2-4.

Example 3c

Next, we're going to explore some bebop-oriented language over our groove.

In the pickup bar of this line, we begin with a *side-stepping* phrase. The four-note phrase spells a Cmaj13 chord (omitting the 3rd), that approaches the Dbmaj7 harmony of bar one from a half step below. This idea briefly spills over into the first couple of notes of bar one, before we transition into the Db Major scale.

The phrasing in bar two here is tricky, with a wide string skip and a rapid position change, so work on this bar in isolation to practice your fingering approach before attempting to play it up to tempo.

For the line that spans bars 3-4, I'm using the C Altered scale, but it is slightly disguised by a couple of chromatic passing notes.

Rhythmically, I chose to use mostly 1/16th notes here to capture the "double time" feel that is characteristic of the bebop style.

Example 3d

Here's another long line that blends the chromatic approach of bebop with arpeggio phrases.

In bar one, after the descending run down, there are two ascending arpeggio phrases on beats 3 and 4. The first spells an Ab6 chord and the second is a Db triad with a leading approach note.

For the long scalic run in bar three that ascends into the higher register, take note of the quick position changes that are needed to keep it flowing smoothly.

Example 3e

Example 3f begins with a long straight 1/16th note phrase played over the Dbmaj7 chord. Here, I'm adding chromatic passing notes to the Db Major scale. In bar two this is contrasted with a slower syncopated phrase that is echoed in bar three. The dotted 1/8th notes in these phrases help to break up the rhythm.

The bluesy line that concludes the lick in bar four borrows the G note from Db Lydian to combine with C Altered to create a weaving melody.

Example 3f

In Example 3g, a long 1/16th note run begins on the "1&" of the bar. In bar one, the Db Major scale is used with some passing notes added. Bar two begins with a Db Lydian scale run that transitions back into Db Major.

I tend to add in melodic leaps to avoid a line travelling in the same direction too often. You can see this most clearly in bar two, between the second and third beats, where I jump to the 14th fret on the first string.

In bar three, over the C7#5 chord, rather than turn to the C Altered scale, this time I switch back to Db Lydian for the descending run. The scale contains a natural 5th rather than the #5 of the harmony, but it still works perfectly well over the C dominant chord.

Example 3g

The next example shows how you can create contrast and variety in your soloing by mixing different rhythms. Over the Dbmaj7 chord in bars 1-2, I chose to syncopate the phrasing by combining 1/16th and 1/8th notes, then introducing 1/8th note triplets.

Next, we move into a long stream of 1/16th notes for the final two bars over the C7#5 chord. It's often good to alter your rhythmic approach at the point of a chord change, as it serves to draw attention to the change in harmony.

Example 3h

Building on the phrasing approach of the previous example, here's another way you can articulate a line with different rhythms over the chord changes.

Over the Dbmaj7 chord here, I play entirely 1/16th notes, but switch to 1/8th note triplets for the C7#5. I also begin to transition into the lower register for the latter chord. It may sound like an obvious thing to do, but moving from high to low, or low to high, is always very effective when building a solo. The listener wants to hear light and shade and contrast in your playing – it tells a story.

Example 3i

Example 3j also combines 1/8th and 1/16th notes to keep things interesting rhythmically. For this lick, I aimed to play a strong opening statement, then leave some space before starting the next phrase.

You'll also hear that to avoid things sounding too staccato with the 1/16th notes, I add in some finger slides in the last two bars for a slightly more horn-like articulation. It's important to add embellishments like this to long lines because it helps them sound more musical – rather than playing with the same attack and dynamic all the time.

Example 3j

Here's a more challenging 1/16th note for you to dig into. It's reminiscent of the type of line the late great Pat Martino would play, who was a master of the long line. Whenever I play a long line like this, I'll hit certain notes harder than others so that they pop out. Varying the dynamics of the line adds a discernible "bounce" to the rhythm of the lick. You only need to add a small amount of emphasis, and for some notes to be fractionally louder than others, to achieve this.

To further enhance the shape of this line, I added melodic leaps every so often (such as bar two, beat 3 and bar three, beats 2 and 3), so that I didn't always play in the same direction.

Example 3k

The next example begins with a Dbmaj7 arpeggio in 8th position. Note the quick position change that is needed at the beginning of bar two, which is achieved via a third finger slide from the 11th to 16th fret.

Bar four features a pedal tone lick, which keeps returning to the root note of C7#5 on the second string, fret 13. The phrasing is a little tricky here as the pedal tone is grouped in seven, before the line ends with a short bluesy 1/16th note phrase. Study the audio, then take this bar slowly to get the exact rhythms.

Example 3l

Here is another fast-picked line that uses odd note groupings to float over the groove – this time a succession of quintuplets (groups of five). The lick is arranged as a repeating motif. In bars 1-2 we cycle around the notes F, Gb and Ab. The F and Ab are both chord tones of Dbmaj7, while the Gb adds the 11th.

Then, we switch to E, F and G at the beginning of bar three. The E note is the 3rd of C7#5, the G is the natural 5th, and the F adds the 11th.

Practice this idea against a modest tempo metronome to make sure you are phrasing the quintuplets accurately.

Example 3m

Example 3n is another long 1/16th note idea that incorporates some quick finger slides and uses chromatic passing notes to maintain the constant forward motion.

To create melodic variety, I utilize some interval leaps in bars 3-4 on non-adjacent strings to break up the flow and structure of the line a little. To learn the line, it can help to break things down into smaller cells of four notes, then combine them.

Example 3n

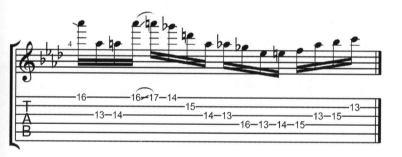

Example 3o begins with a 1/16th note passage before I introduce some ascending tied rhythms in bar two to provide rhythmic contrast. In bar three there are some rapid-picked 1/16th note triplets over the C7#5 chord that include a repeating C pedal tone. The line ends with some quick triplets that move chromatically between Bb and C for an outside-inside effect.

Careful picking and a high degree of accuracy are the order of the day in this line, especially for the fast groups of six in bar three. If this feels like a challenge, spend some time drilling your alternate picking technique in your practice sessions. Without plugging into an amp, you can sit on the couch and watch TV while alternate picking on one string – you'll still be building muscle memory.

Aim for an economical, consistent down-up picking motion, moving the pick only as much as necessary. Try not to lift the pick away from the string, but keep it steady, pushing back and forth through the string as you gradually increase your speed.

Every now and then, push your picking speed to the edge of your ability (even if it sounds awful at first). Over time, the speed and consistency will come.

Example 3o

This line uses a mixture of rhythms to create contrast, beginning with 1/16th notes in bar one and switching to 1/8th notes in bar two. Bar one and the first half of bar two use the Db Major scale to build the line. At the end of bar two, a C major triad is played which anticipates the C7#5 chord that will follow.

In bar three, a 1/4 note triplet is again used to "pull back" the time, before the line concludes with a bluesy lick. Check out the audio to hear the dynamics used in this line. The light and shade keep things engaging for the listener.

Example 3p

While much of Neo-Soul employs silky-smooth phrasing, we can also take a more contemporary jazz approach to create spicier sounding lines, so next up is a line where I was thinking more intervallically.

In bar one, Db Major scale notes are combined with chromatic notes in 3rds and 5ths. For the outside sounding phrase in bar two, I was moving freely between C Major and Db Major scales to create tension and resolution. Rather than execute a simple side-stepping movement, here the two scales are really woven around each other.

In bars 3-4, the same approach is taken but this time combining C Major and C Altered scales, moving freely between them. Further interest is created rhythmically, such as with the 1/16th note quintuplet in bar three.

Example 3q

Example 3r is all about creating drama and excitement by using rapidly changing rhythms. Beginning with a long series of 1/16th notes in the first two bars, I suddenly change course in bar three to heavily punctuated rhythms, which I place in the middle of the bar so that they really stand out.

I also return in bar four to the idea of playing a repeating note motif grouped into 1/16th note triplets, but with a dramatic use of space.

Example 3r

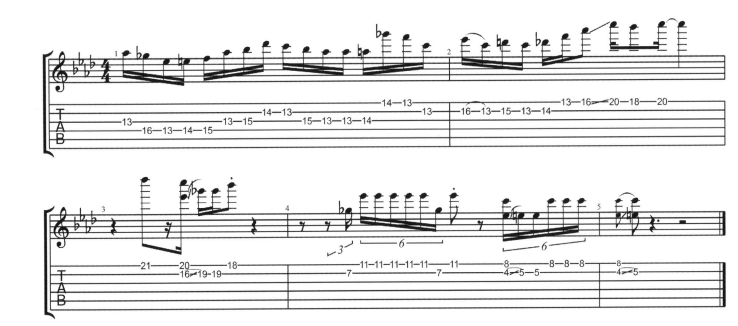

Like many of the previous examples, I'm picking quite hard in Example 3s while still striving to retain good dynamic variety. The line begins with a Db major triad-based motif that is embellished and developed in bar two. In bars 3-4, I continue the Db idea with a Dbmaj7 arpeggio followed by a more scalic line which ascends with the help of some chromatic passing notes.

Example 3s

Example 3t is one of the most rhythmically involved lines so far. You may need to refer to the audio a few times to get my exact phrasing. The aim here was to syncopate the phrasing to achieve a vocal or saxophone-like effect. In Neo-Soul, perhaps more so than any other kind of music, you have the freedom to experiment with rhythm and time. The phrases of many Neo-Soul players will float over the groove just as often as they dig in and play in the pocket.

Example 3t

As in all improvised music, motif development is very important, but it is a strong feature of Neo-Soul. The final line for this chapter illustrates this, especially in bars 3-4. Here I use a motif spread across the first and third strings, which really builds excitement in the solo.

You'll hear how this can work very well alongside the 1/16th note phrases that come before and after the motif. Take care with the final passage which will take you up to the 23rd fret on the first string very quickly!

Example 3u

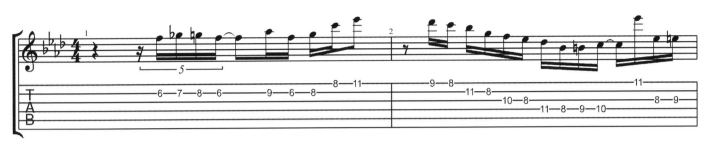

D♭maj7

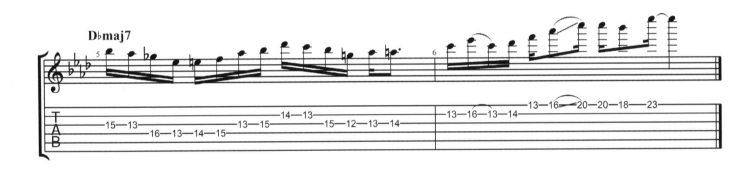

Chapter Four – D Major Groove

In this chapter, we'll be exploring a laidback groove in the key of D Major. This is another tune in which the tonic is avoided, so that the piece has an unresolved feel that never really arrives home. Here is the progression:

| G A | Bm | Em | A |

The use of the IV (G) to V chord (A) movement means that the sequence strongly wants to resolve to the vi (B minor). The second time around, the IV and V chords are replaced by the ii (Em), and in the last bar the V chord serves to turn around the progression.

The overall tonal center of D Major, and the chord choices in the sequence, open up a few possibilities for soloing.

First, because of the central focus of the B minor chord, much of my melodic language here is derived from the B Aeolian scale (B C# D E F# G A) – a D Major scale beginning on the note B. The B Blues scale (B D E F F# A) is also used, which adds the b5 color note (F) into the equation.

In addition, if we look closely at the D Major scale, we discover that it has the notes of three minor pentatonic scales contained within it: B Minor, E Minor and F# Minor Pentatonic. We're all pretty familiar with the basic minor pentatonic shapes, so these simple scales can provide easy access to some solid licks that achieve the sound we want over the harmony.

Chromatic passing notes also feature here too, of course, and usually fall on upbeats rather than downbeats to ground the harmony.

With this in mind, let's look at some licks.

The first example in this chapter uses a three-note harmonic device that is very popular in Neo-Soul and, of course, was popularized way back by my good friend and musical mentor, George Benson.

In the small chord shape, the two outer notes are most commonly played as an octave (as seen in bar one) and the inner note is usually a perfect fifth interval from the root note. As in previous chapters, these figures are played George-style with plenty of sliding articulation to capture the right feel. I end the line by reverting to regular octaves.

Example 4a

The next idea begins with a trill high on the second string before a chromatic run on the same string. This type of idea is really for attention-grabbing dramatic effect, but make sure that you execute it well, paying attention to the slides to keep them clear and distinct.

The line ends with a blues-oriented phrase that combines 1/16th notes in seven then groups of six. This descending lick is another nod to George who often plays with this kind of phrasing.

Example 4b

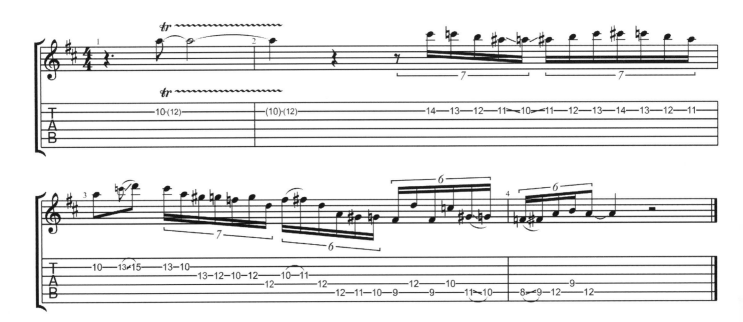

Next, it's time to return to a couple of double-stop ideas. First, a call and response line with double-stops arranged mostly in diatonic 3rds. This is a classic Neo-Soul lick, so listen carefully to the phrasing, which alternates between fluid lines with finger slides and a staccato emphasis. The variation in dynamics helps to give the line a more vocal quality.

Example 4c

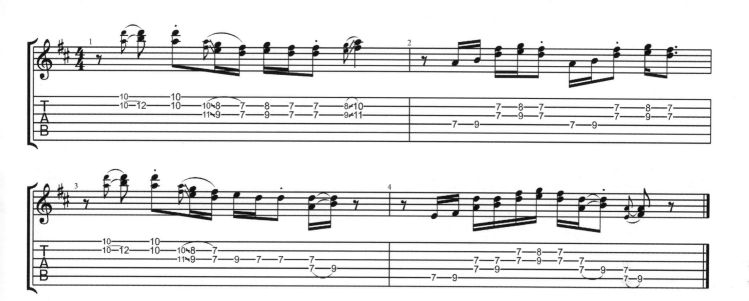

Example 4d continues the call and response motif of the previous lick, but then changes things up in bar four to play a three-over-four feel phrase built from 1/16th note triplets. The run begins on the "2&" of the bar, which can be tricky to count accurately, but listen to the audio a few times to feel where it begins.

Changing rhythmic subdivisions when we want to signal a change in musical mood is a useful tool, because it immediately grabs the listener's attention and lets them know that a new idea is beginning.

Example 4d

Example 4e can be combined with the previous one to create a longer eight-bar line. The three-over-four feel continues in bar one, then in bar two another rhythmic shift occurs as we move away from 1/16th note triplets to straight 1/16ths and more spacious phrasing.

Example 4e

Example 4f is played over the G – A – Bm section of the tune. In this line, chromatic notes help to create an enclosure-type lick in the bar one. Enclosures target a specific chord tone, with scale tones or chromatic notes used to surround (enclose) the target. Here, the targets are the F# note that falls on beat 2, the A note on beat 3, and the D note on beat 4 – all chord tones belonging to Dmaj7.

The main challenge with this line is to nail the phrasing of the different note groupings, which move from five to six to seven-note clusters. Listen to the audio and hear them in the context of the whole line, as well as capturing the dynamics.

Example 4f

Here is another long line which can be challenging to play at full tempo. It cuts against the groove again, with 1/8th note triplets organized into groups of six. It's a very slippery line, so learn it slowly. Work out the optimal fingering to play the notes smoothly, then break them down into smaller cells and learn them separately. Once you have, say, one six-note cell under your fingers, practice the next one, then join the two together. Then add the next cell and work toward mastering each bar in isolation before playing the whole thing.

Example 4g

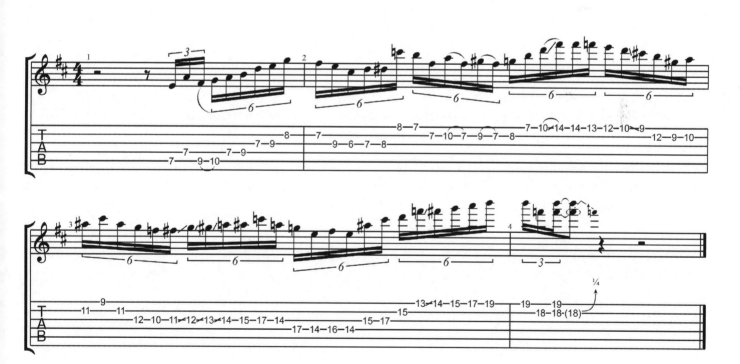

For some light relief, next up we have a textbook jazz-blues phrase that pays homage to George Benson. It shows how successfully blues vocabulary can work in a Neo-Soul setting. Listen carefully to the accompanying audio to understand the phrasing in context and work out your fingering beforehand. It's the type of line that needs to sound relaxed and unforced, sitting slightly behind the beat.

This line can be played in conjunction with Example 4i to make a longer line.

Example 4h

In the sister line to the previous example we combine arpeggio ideas with scalic phrases in typical bebop fashion. In bar one, the D Major scale is sequenced to build an ascending run that targets the G note on the first string, fret 15. The G note implies a Dmaj11 sound.

In bar two, the descending run is another example of the "blended" approach seen earlier. Rather than play an obviously side-stepped line that approaches the D Major tonality from a half step above, the line weaves in and out of D# Major and D Major to produce an outside-inside lick.

We're back in more familiar territory in bars 3-4 with a classic bebop line based around D Major with passing notes used to target the scale tones, the latter falling predominantly on the downbeats to anchor the harmony.

Example 4i

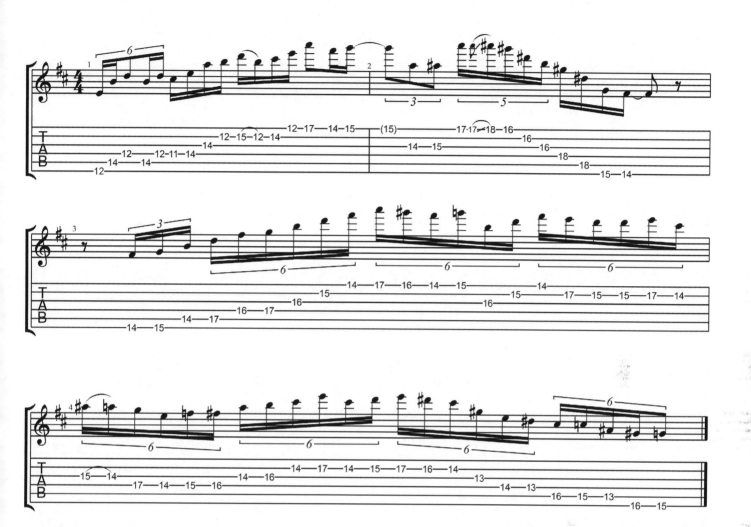

To conclude this chapter, here's a long eight-bar line that incorporates many of the approaches and devices we've seen in previous examples. In the first three bars I've kept my rhythmic phrasing a little sparser to create space, before introducing a long sequence of 1/16th note triplets in bars 4-7.

To close out the line I played a blues-based melody which again features small finger slides. As with many of the above examples, pay particular attention to the dynamics and the small articulations that bring the line to life.

Bars 4-6 pose the biggest challenge, so do break down the phrases into smaller chunks to learn them.

Example 4j

Chapter Five – D Minor Groove

Now we're heading back into a minor vibe and a vamp based on a static Dm7 chord.

Single-chord vamps offer us the most possibilities to stretch out in our solos but can also be more challenging to play over than tunes with lots of changes because they are quite exposing, and it can become obvious when we've run out of ideas!

For the licks in this chapter, I instinctively headed down the road of using the D Blues scale (D F G Ab A C) and D Dorian (D E F G A B C). Many of the lines I play here use these scales as the basic "framework" for the melodic ideas (in terms of their layout on the fretboard) but then I pepper them with chromatic passing notes and enclosure figures, which tends to obscure where one scale ends and another begins. I also occasionally use double chromatic enclosures, where scale notes are targeted with consecutive chromatic notes from above or below.

We'll ease our way into the material with a sparsely phrased line, but don't get lulled into a false sense of security because there are fireworks to follow!

This first line shows how you can begin a solo with fewer notes, but still create musical interest by careful rhythmic placement. The first two double-stops are spaced well apart from each other but are played off the beat, which as you'll hear, makes them sound more dramatic.

After this, I begin to flesh out the line with more continuous phrasing, adding in a Dmin7 arpeggio in bar three to really spell out the harmony. I also make good use of the D Blues scale from beat 3 of the penultimate bar.

Example 5a

Following on from the previous idea, here's a short two-bar phrase that begins with a repeated double-stop played as 1/16th notes. Rather than land on the one, the idea is displaced to beat 2. Bar two is a D Blues scale lick that ends with a double-stop/hammer-on combination.

Example 5b

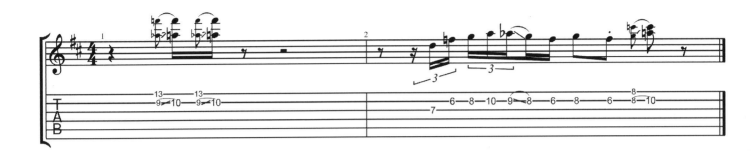

The next line develops the idea that began at the end of the previous example and uses the D Blues scale to create a motif. The free and fluid nature of blues playing means that a whole variety of rhythms come into play. Here, even 1/8ths and 1/16ths contrast phrases built with 1/16th note triplets. Blues phrasing is really about making a strong statement and that's what I was aiming for with this line.

I also emphasize the b5 note of the blues scale a lot in this line, and just that simple addition helps to make the line more soulful and expressive.

Example 5c

Example 5d is another bluesy line but this time combined with the rapid picking that has become a trademark of my playing. The fast-picked motif is built from the D Blues scale. Although each repetition looks similar on paper, each phrase is varied slightly. The whole idea shifts across the bar lines and ends with a triplet-based bluesy lick.

Example 5d

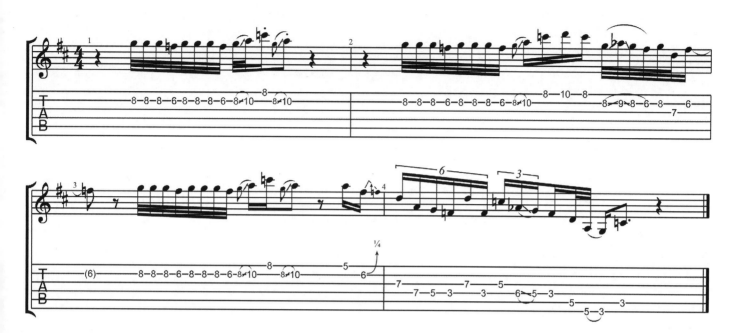

To spice things up, here's a more dramatic and challenging line for you to work through. There are some very fast 1/32nd note passages here, as well as an odd grouping of 1/16th notes at the beginning of bar two.

Learn this one slowly to begin with, working out your hand positions and fingering, then gradually build up the speed. It's important to keep the picking hand very relaxed when playing lines like this, and to not tense up. This can be counter-intuitive, because often our instinct is to dig in and play harder, but this will actually slow you down.

It has been said many times before, "Let the pick do the work", and this means holding it fairly lightly and keeping the wrist nice and loose. Practice picking on just one string to refine your technique.

There is a strong saxophone influence in this line, and to maintain the line's momentum throughout there are lots of chromatic passing notes. Note-wise, the line is a hybrid D Blues and D Dorian line, but I also throw in a Bb note that doesn't belong to either scale. Over the D minor harmony, the Bb creates a #5 sound. Combine this with the b5 of the blues scale and it adds a lot of tension to the line.

Example 5e

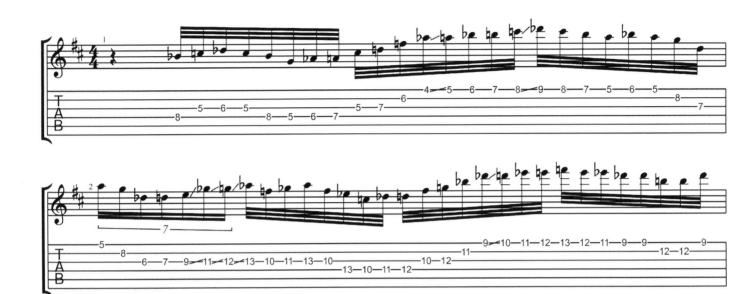

Next we have another line that uses odd note groupings in the phrasing. It looks a little scary on paper, but don't let the groups of nine throw you off. Slow things down and, for practice purposes, think of a group of nine notes as 4 + 5 (or 5 + 4, if you feel the phrase makes more sense that way around).

To me, for example, the first group of nine is best thought of as a 5 + 4 phrase, with the four-note segment being used to navigate onto the first string.

There are also some expressive techniques to look out for in this line, with pull-offs and slides, but focus on the pattern of notes to begin with and add in the articulation later.

Example 5f

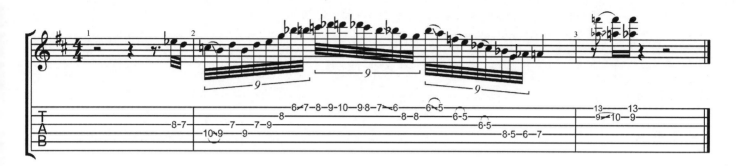

After a quick double-stop lick at the beginning, Example 5g is a long cascading line that rises and falls, filling the gaps with chromatic passing notes. In the second half of bar one, I play a popular four-note bebop phrase that repeats an octave up. It spells an Fmaj7 arpeggio. This short run is aiming for the E note on the first string, fret 12, as its target. Over the D minor harmony, the E gives us a Dm9 sound.

From here, there is a fast chromatic run down, then the line continues to descend until it hits the D root note on the sixth string, 10th fret, at the end of the lick.

Example 5g

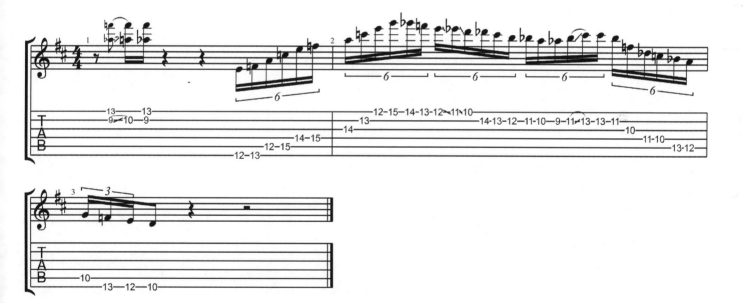

Next up is a blues-based lick that is all about the articulation. The F note (the b3 of Dm7) is emphasized throughout this line. Although it's very bluesy, I mainly used the D Dorian scale here to form the phrases.

Notice the rhythmic variety in this line that keep things sounding fresh. In bar one there is a quick 1/16th note run up, but then a held Bb note slows things down and gradually bends towards the B note of the Dorian scale. Then, after a passage of straight 1/16th notes, 1/8th note triplets pull things back again with that three-over-four feeling in the last bar.

Being able to fluently switch rhythms like this is an important skill to master as an improviser, and it's something you can actively work to improve by jamming over the backing tracks that accompany this book. When working with them, allow yourself to experiment with different phrasing ideas. Take a simple lick, then think of as many ways as you can to apply different rhythmic phrasing.

Example 5h

Example 5i is a long line that contains a number of different approaches and melodic devices. It's a line that goes on a journey as I begin playing quite diatonically, using straight 1/16ths and 1/16th note triplets, then gradually start to use more syncopated, off-beat rhythms as the line develops.

The opening lick is a D Dorian phrase, which is immediately followed up with a D Blues scale lick. Jumping ahead to the final bar, here I use another side-stepping idea. This technique is common to many of the great jazz saxophonists. The idea is to create a short phrase then transpose it up or down to create an outside tension against the harmony.

The phrase begins immediately after beat 1 of bar four and is six notes long. Breaking with the approach used so far, this time I'm playing the D Natural Minor scale.

The transposed phrase begins right on beat 3. Although it looks and sounds as though I have shifted the whole phrase *down*, in fact I've shifted it *up* a half step and the notes here come from the Eb Melodic Minor scale.

Example 5i

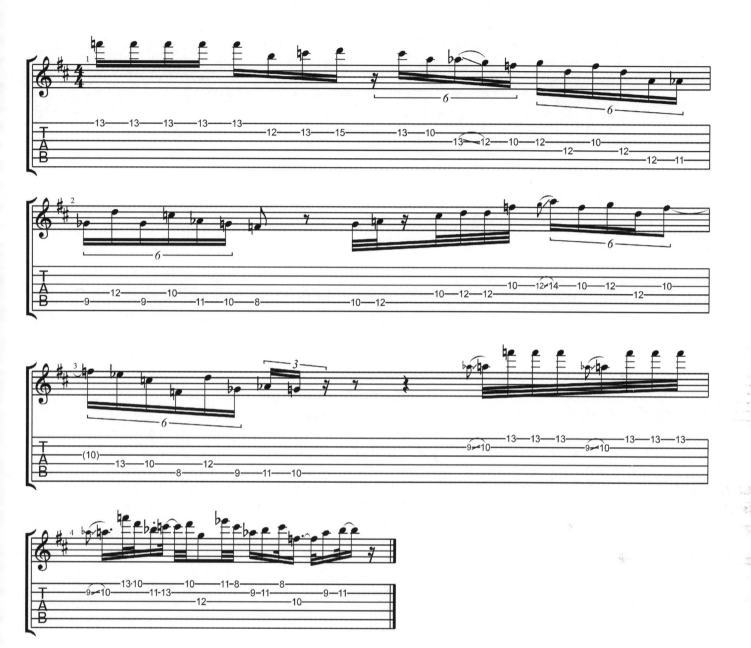

Example 5j opens by repeating the phrase created at the end of the previous example. This time the phrase is shifted upward before the original phrase is restated. This time, however, all the notes belong to D Natural Minor.

As a contrast to the saxophone-like phrasing, the line transitions into more blues-based vocabulary, with triplet rhythms giving the line some swing. The notes are mostly from the D Blues scale.

Example 5j

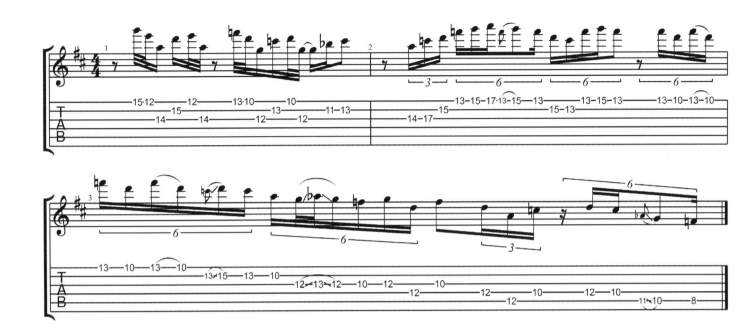

The next couple of examples offer some different ideas to use over our D minor vamp. Drawing inspiration from the playing of Wes Montgomery, the first line is an example of the type of block chord soloing Wes was famous for. The second is an octave lick in the style of George Benson. Wes was equally renowned for playing octaves, of course, but as soon as you hear an octave with the 5th in the middle you think "George!"

In Example 5k I'm mostly using four-note chord structures. Notice that even though I'm soloing with chords, the aim is still to play well-defined phrases that groove over the backing.

The idea in bar one is to approach a rootless Dm9 chord shape on the top strings from a half step below. This repeating idea creates the rhythmic interest.

In bar two, a 5th position Dm11 chord shape is approached from a half step below, then shifted up a whole step to Em11. After this, there is a quick jump up to the higher register to play a less common voicing of Dm9 (this chord could also be viewed as Fmaj13, an effective substitution for D minor). To end the phrase in bar two we have Miles Davis' *So What* movement, from Em11 to Dm11.

In bars 3-4 this entire phrase is repeated but the second half is pulled forward to begin on the "4&" of bar three, rather than the "1&" of bar four.

Example 5k

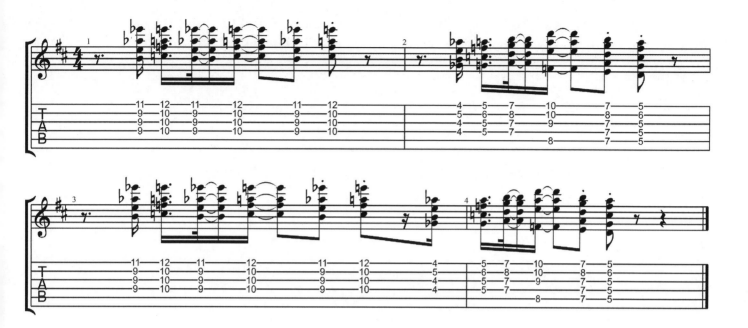

Octaves are a great way to fill out the sound of an arrangement and make strong melodic statements. Again, although octaves can be thought of as an effect, I'm always thinking *melody first, technique second*. In terms of rhythmic placement, I avoid the first beat of each bar until the end. The Benson-style octaves here are used for dynamic emphasis.

Example 5l

Example 5m begins with another repeated note figure before a series of bluesy double stops. Although double-stops are common in soul and blues guitar playing, here I was thinking of a Hammond organ. I recently had the pleasure of working on a Christian McBride big band album with Joey DeFrancesco on keys, and this is just the kind of bluesy phrase that Joey likes to play with a vocal-like quality. It also reminds me of the great Jack McDuff, who I had the privilege of working with very early on in my playing career.

Example 5m

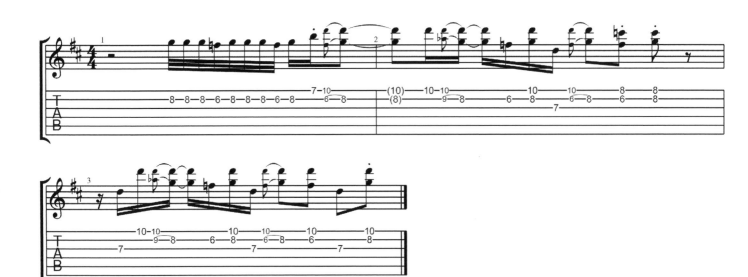

Now we return to a saxophone-like line with Example 5n. This idea reminds me of the wonderful British saxophonist Courtney Pine, who has the ability to play long fluid lines that seamlessly weave in and out of the harmony.

My rhythmic thinking here is mostly around 1/16th note triplets, and instead of just playing scalically, this time I include some arpeggio figures and intervallic leaps. There are also some side-stepping movements here to create tension and resolution.

Example 5n

Here is a similar saxophone-inspired line. It begins with a fast-picked motif in bars 1-2, then moves into a flowing line that requires several position shifts and finger slides to get things sounding smooth. Check out the audio to hear the articulation before attempting it.

I'm thinking D Natural Minor here, but there are a lot of chromatic notes to disguise the scale. To practice this idea, choose a box position scale shape on the neck, hit play on the backing track, and experiment by playing phrases that include both scale tones and passing notes. The key is to visualize the scale shape and keep it in mind at all times.

Example 50

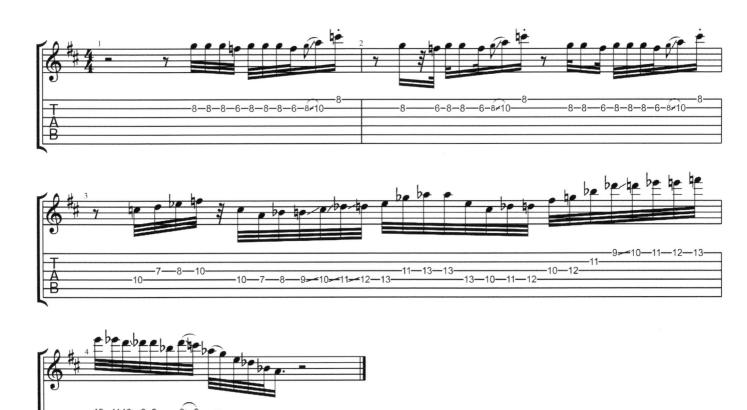

To conclude this chapter, here's one more bluesy riff that creates a motif played on the top two strings. After the dramatic opening, I slow things down and create a lot more space for contrast, and the line ends with a strong bluesy statement.

Example 5p

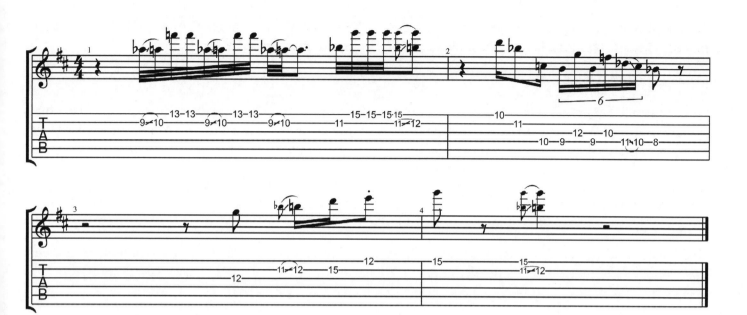

Chapter Six – F Major Groove

To complete our library of licks and phrases, we round things up with a typical Neo-Soul-type groove in the key of F Major. This tune has a very simple two-bar cycle and the chords are:

| Dm7 C Fmaj7 | Bbmaj7 |

Notice that the I chord (Fmaj7) is referenced only fleetingly, on beat 4 of bar one. Instead, the main focal points of the music are the Dm7 and Bbmaj7 chords. Though our overriding tonal center is F Major (and lots of these lines are F Major scalic ideas), I learned a long time ago that while it's good to be aware of the key of a tune, it's more musical to react to each chord in the moment.

Think of it this way: although Dm7 and Bbmaj7 are diatonic to F Major, we can view them as tonal centers or simply "sounds" in their own right, and this will influence the kind of melodic ideas we play over them.

The purpose of the lines in this chapter is to show how you can build ideas from very simple motifs, then expand them into more challenging ideas. Let's start with a bluesy statement that uses the F Major scale (F G A Bb C D E) with an Ab passing note borrowed from the F Blues scale (F Ab Bb B C Eb).

Example 6a

Staying in the same zone of the fretboard, we can embellish our basic phrase by adding articulation – in this case some sliding double-stops. Notice that the main phrase of Example 6a on the second and third strings retains its shape.

Example 6b

Example 6c builds on the previous idea and takes it forward. The notes are different this time, but it's important to note that the *shape* of the phrase is very similar. Once again, the notes come from the F Major scale with an added Ab note.

Example 6c

Now we can take the phrase in a slightly new direction and move away from the 8th position zone we've been playing in. Bar one is straight F Major scale, but in bar two a couple of passing notes spice up the harmony. We've already used the Ab note in previous examples, but now a Gb is introduced.

A device some blues players use is to play a lick that includes the b9 of the tonic chord. Our tonal center is F Major, so in this case Gb is the b9. It's a surprising but nice tension note, and the phrase is quickly resolved to end on an F note.

Example 6d

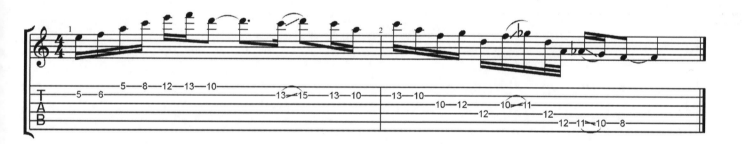

After the contrast of the previous phrase, we can return to the same zone of the neck and hint again at the motif that began this exploration of ideas. Returning to a motif is a great way to connect with your listeners and adds the vital storytelling element to your solos. Motifs are a great way to develop a theme throughout your solo – an approach that has been used from the great classical composers onwards.

Example 6e

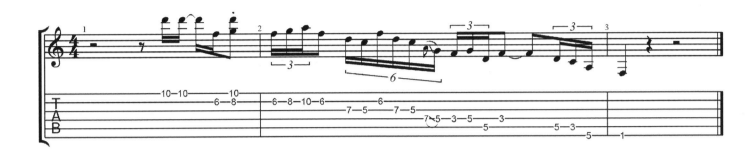

Next we have a much longer line that takes the theme and elaborates on it. Notice the recurring phrase on the second string that emphasizes the main notes from our very first motif. This phrase could be played in endless different ways, just by varying the rhythm and placement of the notes.

Example 6f

Now it's time to introduce a new idea that we can take and build upon. In bar one of Example 6g I play a new motif. It's an ascending run that ends with an interval jump. The first eight notes are the same four-note phrase played in two octaves, then the pattern is broken as we play a bebop-style enclosure lick on the first string, the target of which is the Bb on fret 6. From the Bb we skip a string to play a D note to create a 6th interval.

This example highlights an important idea in jazz – that of transposing licks to different zones of the fretboard. Listen to the lick and you'll hear that the phrase in bar one sounds very "inside", the phrase in bar two sounds "outside" the harmony, and in bar three we're back inside. Let's take a close look at what's happening here, relative to our tonal center of F Major.

In bar one, all the notes come from the F Major scale, apart from the B note on the first string, fret 7, which is a passing note used to create the enclosure lick.

In bar two, the motif of bar one has been transposed up a minor third (a distance of three frets), note for note. The shape of the phrase is identical to before, but now we're playing outside of the harmony, effectively in the key of Ab Major. At this point in the tune a Bbmaj7 chord is playing underneath and the results of this superimposed harmony are interesting.

Rather than producing a whole series of clashing notes, the line suggests extended or altered tones over the Bbmaj7 chord. Looking at the first few notes, the C implies the sound of Bbmaj9, the Db is the #9, and the F is the 3rd of Bbmaj7. Then, the Eb on the first string, fret 11, implies a Bbmaj11 sound, and so on.

In bar three, we shift the whole phrase up another minor third and suddenly we're back inside the harmony. All the notes come from F Major (apart from that one chromatic note), but we are just accessing the scale beginning from an E note instead of the A note we began with in bar one.

If you've never thought about doing something like this, it's worth exploring the idea in your practice sessions. The minor third shift is a very common idea in modern jazz and lends itself well to the arena of Neo-Soul.

Example 6g

71

The next example begins with the same motif but modifies it on the first string. From here, the line takes a different direction altogether, but the fact that we began the line with the same idea gives the line a sense of continuity and creates a connection to the previous idea.

You can hear that the phrasing is similar throughout, but more chromatic notes have been added to give the line a more bebop flavor.

Example 6h

The next long line begins with the transposed motif from bar three of Example 6g, then develops the idea in that zone of the fretboard. This line uses chromatic passing notes to weave inside and outside the harmony, eventually resolving back to the F tonic note.

Example 6i

Example 6j expands on the ascending motif idea but combines two ideas to change things up a bit. First of all, in bar one we make it more bluesy by adding articulation in the form of slides and varying the rhythm with 1/8th note triplets.

Then, in bar two, the rhythm is altered more radically with a fast ascending run arranged as 1/16th note sextuplets. If you find this tricky at first, break it down into groups of three notes and play it slowly to learn the shape of the line.

Example 6j

The next example begins with a variation of the ascending motif line we've used in previous examples, then goes off to explore that zone of the neck, peppering the line with chromatic passing notes. I'd love to say that I have a rock-solid theoretical explanation for a line like this, but the truth is, sometimes I'm just exploring a sound and seeing where it will lead me!

It's perfectly fine to experiment like this. The main thing to remember, if you're going to play outside, is to have a *clear target* to aim for that will bring you back inside in due course. In bar two, for example, which is played over a Bbmaj7 chord, the line begins and ends on a D note (the 3rd of Bbmaj7). Bar three, played over a Dm7 chord begins on a B note, suggesting a Dm13 harmony, and ends on the D root note.

In bars 5-6, the line is grounded by bringing it firmly back into its F tonality with a bluesy line that provides a solid contrast to the earlier chromaticism.

Example 6k

In bar one of the next example, we reverse the minor third transposition idea used earlier. This time, instead of starting inside and transposing to move outside the harmony, we're beginning outside and moving back in. The target is the A note on the first string that falls on beat 3 and starts a phrase that spells a D minor triad. In the latter half of bar two, we transpose back up (the phrase that begins on the first string, fret 8, spells an F minor triad). Bars 3-4 bring it home again with a grounded bluesy lick.

Example 6l

Example 6m continues this melodic line of thought in bar one, before we launch into another bebop-inspired line that goes outside and inside the harmony.

Again, though the line sounds complex, we can break it down by looking at the target notes that helped form the line. In bar three, for example, the chromatic run up on the first string (played over Dm7) hits an F note on fret 13 on beat 2, and is the b3 of the chord. After some more passing notes, we hit an E note at the end of bar two (the 9th of D minor), which leads chromatically into the next phrase. Similarly, in bar five, the chromatic ascent targets the root note of Dm7 on the first string, fret 10.

Example 6m

In the next example, our original motif is referenced briefly in bar one, played over a Bbmaj7 chord. As the sequence rolls around again, starting with a Dm7 chord in bar two, there is a new idea – a fast-picked passage that incorporates a sliding double-stop. Notes on the second string act as pedal tones underneath the repeating F note on the first string (the b3 of Dm7). It's the type of lick George Benson famously pioneered and works really well over a static tonal center.

In bar three we're back to the Bbmaj7 chord and a line with chromatic passing notes. The main feature of this line is that it borrows the B note from the F Blues scale to add tension to the underlying harmony and create a bluesy bebop line.

In bar four, the line played over Dm7 contains lots of passing notes, but you can probably visualize here that I am just taking advantage of playing across adjacent strings around 12th/14th position, aiming for the C note (the last note in the bar), which is the b7 of Dm7 and leads chromatically into the closing phrase.

Example 6n

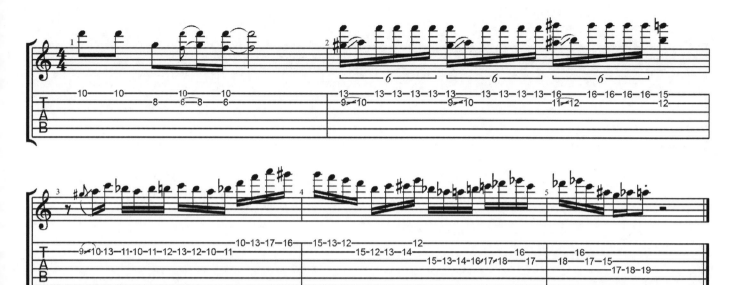

Here's another chromatic positional lick for you to try. Again, there are lots of passing notes in this line and some outside-sounding melodies, but I stay in 12th position for the majority of the lick, breaking out only at the end to bring the melodic line back inside with a bluesy phrase. Notice that the note choices are heavily influenced by the position I'm playing in at that moment.

Example 60

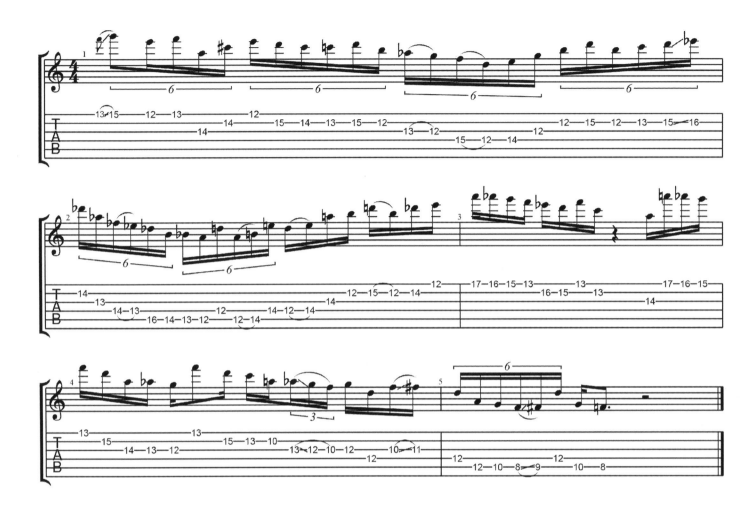

Here is a more dramatic example of note targeting: where we begin at one point and have a destination point in mind. The long descending run in bar one begins with a sliding double-stop that emphasizes a G note (implying a Dm11 sound over the Dm7 harmony). Thereafter, the goal of the line is to get to the D root note on the sixth string, fret 10, on beat 1 of bar two. Slow this line right down to learn the shape of it.

Example 6p

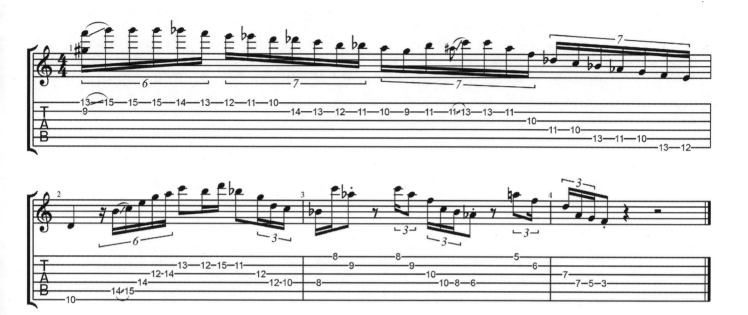

Example 6q features another rapid-picked pedal tone idea. Bar two has a similar idea to the one used in Example 6n, then we move into the sequenced line that spans bars 3-4.

Play the lick in bar two by holding down the 13th fret on the first string with the fourth finger, then use the first finger only to fret the notes on the second string, sliding into each one.

For the sequenced line in bars 3-4, you'll need all four fingers. Hold down the D note on the first string, fret 10, with the fourth finger and keep it in place. The first, second and third fingers will play the notes on frets 6, 8 and 9 respectively. The first finger will hop over onto the third string to play the D note on fret 7. Learn the movements slowly before bringing the lick up to speed.

Example 6q

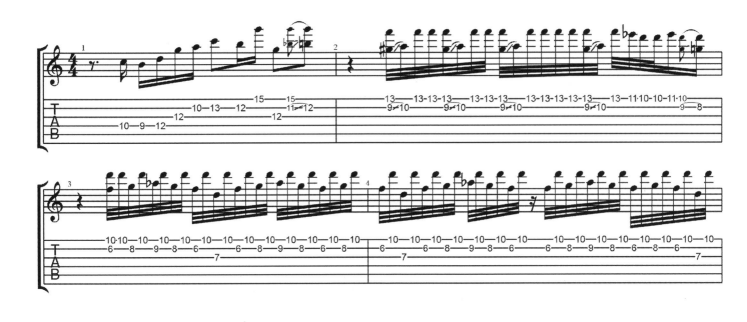

We round things off with a final bluesy line that combines descending and ascending runs, passages of 1/16th note triplets and ends with three "So What" chords that lead to a Dm11. Check it out!

Example 6r

Conclusion

I hope you've enjoyed exploring some of the cool vibes of Neo-Soul. The mercurial nature of this music (is it soul, jazz, gospel, funk?) allows us a great deal of latitude when improvising. Soulful, bluesy licks will always go down well, but we can also stretch out with bebop-inspired chromaticism over the open tonal centers.

Let me end where we began with a reminder of the main tools at the disposal of the Neo-Soul guitarist:

Blues licks – Blues licks, injected with lots of soul and feel are go-to ideas in Neo-Soul. Aim for behind-the-beat phrasing and focus on call and response licks, as well as vocal-like articulation.

Double-Stops – They work especially well in this kind of music to fill out the sound and provide a strong sense of rhythm.

Motifs – a key skill in many styles of music is creating "connected" musical ideas that follow a theme. Invest practice time into developing motifs and you'll always grow as a player. Motival playing is essential for telling a story with your solos.

Rhythmic phrasing – Neo-Soul is all about the groove, and over the typically expansive, open chord changes it's important to bring some rhythmic variety. Remember, too, that you can get lots of mileage out of one simple lick by varying the rhythm.

Long lines – Long melodic lines have their place in Neo-Soul, and allowing your lines to flow across the bar line will make your ideas sound less predictable.

Chromatic passing notes – An idea borrowed from jazz is to target specific notes and approach them from above or below with chromatic and extended passing notes. Think Charlie Parker and any players from the bebop tradition. Remember that you can take a lot of liberties with this idea as long as you keep the "home" tonality of the tune in mind. Playing longer chromatic lines is a great way to create an outside-inside sound, as long as you resolve your idea to a strong chord tone.

One final piece of advice I want to pass onto you is that when you play any melodic idea, begin and end with *intent*. Expressing ourselves musically is like having a conversation. Ask yourself this: what kind of communicator most grabs your attention – the person who speaks clearly and expresses their ideas with clarity, or the person who mumbles their way through a conversation and never really gets to the point? It can be hard work to listen to the latter, right? But a great communicator will always command our attention.

It's a journey we're all on as musicians: to get better at transferring onto our instrument what we hear in our head. To improve this skill, shut the door to your practice room and try singing melodic lines, then playing what you hear. The more you work at this, the more you'll narrow the gap between what you *want* to play and what you *actually* play. An added bonus is that you'll play much clearer musical lines that have intent, purpose and direction.

Enjoy your playing and keep exploring!

Mark.

Made in the USA
Coppell, TX
13 August 2022

81383045R00048